A little piece of England

The hill station of Nuwara Eliya

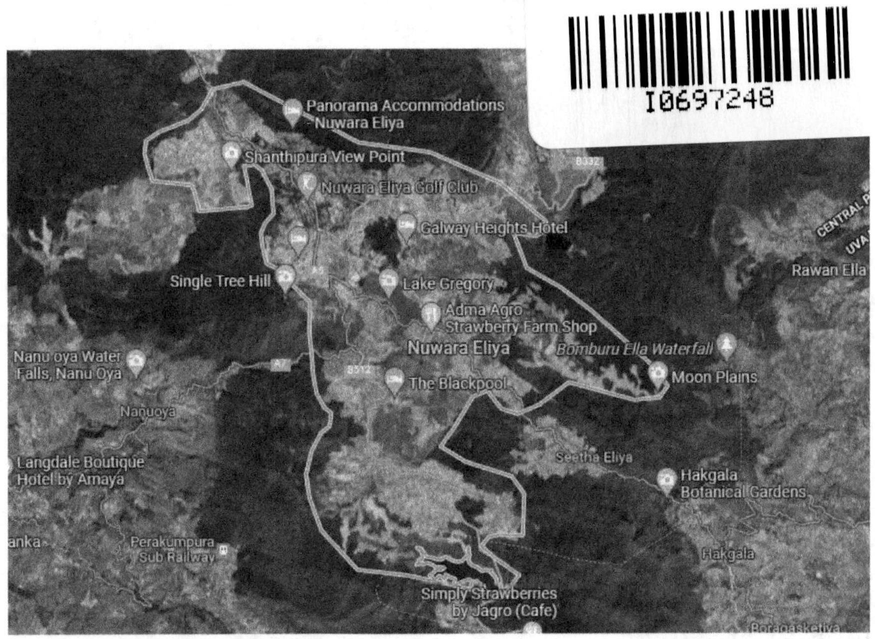

Fazli Sameer

Sameer, Fazli
A little piece of England / Fazli Sameer, - Colombo 2022
ISBN 979-843-05491-0-7

1.   Sociology, English

A Little Piece of England
Fazli Sameer
Colombo, Sri Lanka

to my two lovely daughters,
Melina & Nadia

First Print - 2022
ISBN: 979-843-05491-0-7
Published by: Fazli Sameer, Colombo, Sri Lanka
Cover/Graphic Design: Fazli Sameer
Printed by : KDP/my cloudreader

All proceeds from the sale of the paperback and eBook
editions will be donated to the Bambarakelle SOSVillage
in Nuwara Eliya

Contents

Introduction

The name, "Nuwara Eliya", (**Sinhala**: නුවර එළිය [nuwərə ɛlijə]; **Tamil**: நுவரெலியா) means "city on the plain (table land)" or, in another interpretation, "city of light". It has always been famous for its picturesque landscape and temperate climate. It is bounded by Kandapola in the north, Nanu Oya in the west, Hakgala in the South, and Uda Pusselawa in the east.

Located at an altitude of 1,868m (6,128 ft), from sea level, the city was considered to be the most important location for tea production in old Ceylon.

The city is overlooked by "Pidurutalagala", the tallest mountain in Sri Lanka and is known for its soothing cool climate – the coolest locality in the whole island.

Prior to its discovery by Dr. John Davy in 1819, Nuwara Eliya was already home to an illustrious history that showcased ruins of ancient irrigation systems and stone inscription that dated as **far back as 900AD and 1000AD**

School days in Colombo in the 60s were filled with a mixture of study, commuting, cricket, and homework.

The school year was divided into three terms at the end of which we were given a 4 week holiday to rest and recuperate from the rigors of blackboard, chalk, and dusters.

The one that we looked forward most to was the August holidays that popped up immediately after the end of the second term.

This was Nuwara Eliya season for us young urchins in Colombo.

It was this time of the year when the family used to start preparations to take that holiday up in the hills in the quaint little town that is so reminiscent of England. Most Colombo families took their summer holidays in Nuwara Eliya in April where lots of activities were available in the town for the family. But the overcrowded environment was too always too much for us to join the party during this season. Hence we always chose August, where the crowds were less even though the weather was much colder.

The family group gathered at 298 in Bambalapitiya, where my paternal grandparents lived and then set out to the Fort Railway Station to catch the night mail express train to Nanu Oya, the closest railway station to access Nuwara Eliya.

Trains have always fascinated me since childhood, and the whole ride up to the hills, approximately 210+ km, usually lasted for a little more than 6.5 hours. Notable stops along the way were Ragama, Veyangoda, Mirigama, Polgahawela, Rambukkana, Kadugannawa, Peradeniya, Gampola, Nawalapitiya, Watawala, Rozelle, Hatton,

Talawakele, Watagoda, Great Western, Nanu Oya.

From Nanu Oya station we had to take the bus to Nuwara Eliya town.

Nanu Oya Railway Station

The ride from Nanu Oya Railway Station to Nuwara Eliya town was a perilous one, with the cold air hitting us from all corners of the sky and the bus rolling on its edge up and down many hills and dales.

One feels a great sense of relief and contentment on reaching the town after a long and tiring train ride from Colombo. The cool and salubrious climate also contributes to the comfort amid a serene, green, and lush environment all around.

The Town

The town of Nuwara Eliya is located in the tea country hills of central Sri Lanka. The naturally landscaped Hakgala Botanical Gardens displays roses and tree ferns, and shelters monkeys and blue magpies. Nearby Seetha Amman Temple, a colorful Hindu shrine is decorated with many religious figures. Densely forested Galway's Land National Park is a sanctuary for endemic and migratory bird species, including bulbuls and flycatchers.

Nuwara Eliya Town has always had its glamour with its beautifully carpeted green, colorful flowers blooming, and the old colonial buildings standing tall like edifices from the past.

Most of the folks living in other parts of the coastal belt, where the weather is hot, humid, and tropical, throughout the year, choose to drive up, ir even hop the train, to Nuwara Eliya, to enjoy their vacations.

The cooler climate, salubrious environment, fresh food, and tranquility that the town afforded were relished very much by these city dwellers.

Hotel and guest house accommodation, in the 60s, was not so abundant as what it is today. Hence, most people used the facilities of holiday bungalows that belonged to friends and family.

These homes were fully furnished and also had the facility of a cook who lived in the premises and doubled up as a watchman.

The residences were taken care of immaculately and the gardens and foliage were well nourished and lifted up the environment of the homes tremendously. A break from the rigors of a 9 to 5, clock chasing, working life in Colombo up to the hills of Nuwara Eliya was very much like therapy for the weary body and mind.

Many places of interest in the town attracted the visitors to drive to, or even walk by, and enjoy the glamour and glitz that they offered to these hungry "tourists".

The Park, Grand Hotel, Racecourse, Lake Gregory, Horton Plains, Worlds End, Moon Plains, Strawberry farms, and many other locations were much sought after.

Streets of Nuwara Eliya

Badulla Road (A5)

The A5 road is a main thoroughfare that connects Peradeniya to Chenkalady. It is also referred to as the PBC Highway, short for "Peradeniya-Badulla-Chenkalady".

The highway passes through Geli Oya, Gampola, Pusselawa, Nuwara Eliya, Keppetipola, Welimada, Hali-Ela, Badulla, Passara, Lunugala, Bibile, Padiyanthalawa, Maha Oya, Thumpalancholai, Karaidiyanaru, and ends at Chenkalady.

Queen Elizabeth Drive

Is the section of the PBC Highway that cuts through Nuwara Eliya Town.

St Andrews Road

Starts at Park Road, in the heart of town, and treks all the way up north to reconnect to the PBC Highway.

Waterfield Drive

Branches off to the east from St Andrews Drive and moves up north to Jetwings hotel.

Keena Road, travels north east from Cross Street.

Cross Street, the Golf Green City Bungalow ro Keena Road.

Bandaranaike Mawatha, starts in the center of town and moves up north towards St Andrews Road.

Chapel Street

Hill Street

Rahula Road

Lady McCallum Drive

Sri Jayathileke Mawatha

Gemunu Mawatha

Police Lane

Kanagaratnam Road

Grand Hotel Road

Lawson Road

New Bazaar Road

Park Road

Old UdaPusselawa Road

Buddha Jayanthi Mawatha

Mount Mary Road

Church Road

Mount Mary Road

Rajasinghe Mawatha

Sri Sumangali Mawatha

Glenfall Road
Lebonen Road

Ranasinghe Mawatha

Unique View Road

Haddon Hill Road

Holiday Bungalow Road

Single Tree Road

Shirin Road

Lower Gibson Road

Upper Gibson Road

Kelegalla Road

Kalukele Road

Lady Horton Road

St Anne Road

Upper Lake Road

Havelock Road

Burrows Road

Vajira Mawatha

Homes

Many are the luxurious bungalows and homes that were owned by the rich and famous from other parts of the island. These were used as holiday homes for the owner's families and also friends.

"Barnes Hall"

Sir Edward Barnes, governor from 1824 to 1831 built his home known as "Barnes Hall" which is today called the Grand Hotel. From 1831 - 1837 the governor was Sir William Horton who had written many articles about Nuwara Eliya in his many literary works In 1838 Samuel Baker, an explorer, discovered Nuwara Eliya as a place with the exact climate of England and made it into a retreat for the British colonists to retire and relax and indulge in hunting which as a favorite past time. He also introduced farming during this time.

"Bakers Farm"

Mr Samuel Baker was also instrumental in building "Baker's Farm, a hospital ward at the Nuwara Eliya base hospital known today as Bakers Ward. He returned to England in 1866 due to ill health. However, recognition of his work at Nuwara Eliya the broadest water fall in Nuwara Eliya was named after him and is called " Bakers Falls:'

"Bloomfield"

The first Sri Lanka to own property was the father of late SWRD Bandaranayake, in 1910. SWRD' house was overlooking the racetrack on the hill.

"Cheltanham", owned by the Macan Markar family is located on top of a hill a few meters out of town.

The Royal College 42nd Group Scout Platoon used to make its annual camp to Nuwara Eliya and used this large and glamorous facility to stay in. The house had a long walkway down a steep incline that led to a green patch of grass that served as an ideal play ground for cricket, rugby, and football. The stairway and upper floor was all constructed of wood.

As young and energetic boy scouts we always enjoyed the ambience of the large house in all its splendor and magnificence in those early years in the 60s.

Today, it has been converted into a boutique hotel called "Cheltanham Cottages"

"Rosy Lodge" owned by the WM Hassim family was located at the rear of Cargills on Lady McCallum Drive. The house was flanked by two homes, one belonging to former mayor and MP, the late Jabir A Cader, and the other owned by the late MH Mohamed, ex Speaker of the House and ex MP/Minister.

Many were the happy hours we have spent at Rosy Lodge, as the owners belonged to my wife's extended family and hence we had easy access to it whenever we wanted to take the ride up to the hills.

"Unique View", #22 opposite municipality, close to Grosvenor hotel.

"Blackpool", located on the Horton Plain road south of the town. Now converted to a tourist guest house

"Yalta", owned by the Shums and Co. family overlooked Lake Gregory in N'Eliya.

"Qauser al Hana", Was bought by the late Falil A Caffoor, MP. for his wife and was located adjacent to "Yalta"

"Labukelle" owned by the Esufali family

"Clovelly" Hussain Caffoors maternal uncle, the late ULMM Mohideen bought this bungalow from Mr Fernando of Negombo.

It was purchased for the protection & migration of his family from Colombo to N'Eliya to be safe from the air raids by the Japanese in around 1945/1948

"Watermead", located on the Badulla Road, was built by the British residents in keeping with the architectural style of rural England.

"The Paynter Home", located on Gemunu Mawatha was started, by the Rev Arnold Paynter, in 1924. It was previously called The Nuwara Eliya Childrens' Home.

Arnold Paynter, born in 1897, is the son of the Rev AS Paynter (UK) & Agnes Louis Paynter (Sri Lankan) who were, both, very active missionaries in old Ceylon.

His siblings are Ada Paynter, David Paynter and Eva Paynter.

It was when Arnold started accompanying his missionary mother on her visits to the villages in the Uva province that he first observed and was moved with the problems faced by the impoverished kids there.

He first lived in the village for a period of two years and then set up a school for the kids there. These children 'ran wild in the tea plantations', (his own words) and were very much in need of a home where they could be raised good human beings, learning the English language too in the process. This was the catalyst that led to the establishment of the Paynter Home.

"Noorani Villa", located at the rear of Cargills on Lady McCallum Drive.

"New Devon Cottage", located on Lady McCallum Drive

"Burnside", FB De Mels house

"Hill Dale", located at Kuda Oya in Labukelle

"White Vintage Cottage",

"Longden", is located on the Badulla Colombo Highway in Nuwara Eliya.

"Queenswood Cottage", is located on the Badulla Road.

"The Queensbury", located at 6 Chapel Street.

"Balnacoyle" presently the brewery, was previously owned by the Asgeraly family

"Molesworth", located at the rear of Glendover was a bungalow in 1920

"Hilldale"

"Kent Cottage", located at Lot 6 in Little England Cottages

"Hummingbird Hill"

"The Westbury", located at 17 Udapussalawa Road.

"Stafford", built in 1884, now re-established as Stafford Bungalow (2013), is a family owned home which has been in existence for more than 130 years. It was originally owned by a Scottish planter and is located amidst a working tea estate in the village of Ragala. It is located on Grand Hotel Road, in the center of town.

"Glendevon", is presently converted to a hotel, and, was a tea company office in 1948, according to the pictures on the wall. It has very beautiful English gardens immaculately kept around its environs and the old colonial charm is very visible within its premises.

A significant aspect of this place is the vintage snooker table, built in the 19 century that is more than 135 years old that stands in the billiard room above the bar.

"Hillcrest"

"Lady Horton", is located on Lady Hortons Walk on Bona Vista Road.

"Brockenhurst", is located at 98 Waterfied Drive.

"The Forest & Lake"

"Lynden Grove", located on Glenfall Road, off the Grand Hotel, a bungalow previously owned by Mansoor A Cader, is presently a boutique hotel managed by his grand daughter and her husband.

"Rosedale", is located at Kellagalla Road.

"Grace" is located on Cross Road.

"Seven Oaks", is located on Keena Road.

"Wintry Hills" is located on Toppass.

"Hamlyn", is located on Windenere Park.

"Victoria", is located in Bambarakelle.

"Oliphant"

"Pedro View" is located in Vajirapura, Boralanda.

"Sherwood" is located at 22 Sherwood.

"Ferncliff", located at 10 Wedderburn Road.

"Albany"
"Rosedale"
"Eden Grand", located in Hospital Quarters

"Adisham"

"Greenhill"

Places of interest

The Windsor Hotel was at one time acquired by the Colombo Colonial Hotel family. The entire hotel was refurnished by them to a very good standard. There was a Burger musician named Stuart who was married to their daughter, who was installed as the General Manager of the Hotel. Stuart, being a top class Musician, used to play host to many western musicians who used to visit N Eliya. The bar and billiard room were patronized by many folks who lived in Nuwara Eliya and the visitors in town.

The Grand Hotel, located on Grand Hotel Road, has always been the premier star class facility in town since 1819.

Many are the celebrities and people in high places who have stayed in this hotel and enjoyed its excellent service and offerings.

There are a few hotels in the East which command the advantages of this well-known hostelry. It is located 6,200 ft above sea level, enshrouded by a magnificent climate, and in very close proximity to golf links which are claimed, by experts, to be the best east of the Suez.

There is excellent trout fishing in the localityanmd visitors to the hotel will find themselves in ver close proximity to the bus station, taxi stands, park, post office, race course, department store, clubs, and bazaar. Mr Loesch, the manager during Briotish Colonial times, has had great experience as a caterer. He was, previously, the manager of a hotel in Hamburg, in Germany, and also served in th services as a purser in the Hamburg American Company.

Since he undertook the management of the facility, the Grand Hotel has doubled its size on his persistent representations, and this expansion has been totally justiofied by the results that have been observed, thereafter.

Further improvement to expand the hotel to cater to 200 people with 120 bedrooms has also been planned. The building will have two floors with most of the bedrooms located on the upper floor.

The drawing room and dining hall area will cover 2,500 sqft.

A. LOESCH.
(Manager, Grand Hotel.)

An electric plant will be installed to supply the facility with power. The bathrooms and conveniences will be laid out in the most modern design with hot and cold water facilities and tiled walls and floors. The hotel stands on 17 acres of land, with 7 acres of kitchen and garden, with a private dairy conveniently located on higher ground.

[Twentieth Century Impressions of Ceylon by Arnold Wright p833]

Grand Hotel, Nuwara Eliya

"Ramayana"

The Ramayana, the Indian mythological epic relates how King Ravana, of Lanka, abducted Sita, the wife of Rama, in India, and took her back to Sri Lanka. It is believed that the Ravana had his capital in Nuwara-Eliya ("the glade with the city") and that he kept Sita captive in Sita Eliya. ("The glade of Sita"). Today there is a Hindu temple on this location (The famous Hakgala Botanical Garden is situated closer to this temple). The mythological story goes that an army of monkeys of Rama was sent to save Sita from her captivity. Hanuman, the leader of this army was punished by Ravana, by setting fire to his tail. Legends claim that Hanuman burnt the entire district of Nuwara-Eliya with his flaming tail. The black soil, which forms a top layer in this region is supposed to be composed of the ashes of the city.

"Seetha Amman Kovil" (Hindu Temple)

Located in Seetha Eliya, about a kilometer away from the Hakgala Botanical Gardens and 5 km from Nuwara Eliya town. It is believed to be the location where Seetha was held captive by Ravana as told in the Ramayana mythology stories.

"There is a rock on the opposite bank where Sita sat and meditated. Also this Ashoka forest is a clear indication that she came here when she was brought to Lanka," said G.T. Prabhakaran, who is in charge of the temple.

There is also a belief that at a particular point in the stream, the water has no taste. "This is the spot she cursed. You cannot drink the water. Drink it further downstream," one temple worker said. Temple workers are keen to show visitors the spot where Sita bathed, the stone she sat on and where she prayed. Beliefs here are evidently strong and devotees are convinced that this episode of the Ramayana epic did indeed take place here.

"Labukelle Tea Factory"

"The Hill Club", located on Grand Hotel Road, is a gentleman's club which was established in 1876 by a British coffee planters, WH Walker, J Wickwar, and H Saunders in the town. It was initiated with only a bar and a billiard room. The first president of the club was Edward Rosling, elected to office in 1899. The present facility came into existence in the 1930s, constructed by the British contracting company, M/S Edward, Reid & Begg.

The club was originally meant for males only and ladies were, subsequently, allowed to join in 1967.

"Victoria Museum"

Victoria Museum is located on the Uda Pusselawa Road.

"The Racecourse"

Horse racing was introduced to Nuwara Eliya by John Baker, the brother of Samuel Baker. The racecourse was established in the 1840s where English horses were trained to run.

Racecourse, Nuwara Eliya

The inaugural race meeting at Nuwara Eliya was held in 1875 and was organised by the Nuwara Eliya Gymkhana Club. These meetings carried on intermittently until 1900 when the current race course was laid out.

"Post Office"

The Nuwara Eliya Post Office, located on Queen Elizabeth Drive, is an elegantly constructed, Tudor styled red brick and wall edifice that has been standing since 1894.

Samuel Godfried Koch

Mr SG Koch was the Post & Telegraph Master at the Nuwara Eliya Post Office is a member of a very old Dutch Burgher family descendant from the 17 century. Born in Jaffna on Oct 23 1862 and joined the telegraph department after completing his high school education. The department was then operated by the Indian Telepgraph Office.

S. G. KOCH.

SG Koch   After serving as a signaler for eleven years, he was appointed deputy Telegraph Master at Kandy in 1891, and after having served in various other departments in different locations in the island he was selected to serve at the Nuwara Eliya Post Office.

Twentieth Century Impressions of Ceylon by Arnold Wright p836

Single Tree Hill, a hilltop with mountain and a great view of the sunset

Grosvener Hotel, on Haddon Hill Road, is a colonial style home that is now a holiday resort that was built at the British colonial times for British governor. It was converted to a hotel in the late 70's.

St Andrews Hotel, is located on St Andrews Road and was first constructed in 1875 as part of land gifted to a British colonial civil servant by the Crown. The place later became The Scots Club. It was only in 1891 that it got its name as St Andrews and was managed by Mr Humbert.

The hotel was bought over in 1918 by Arthur Edward Ephraums, after which it was expanded to have an extra wing and two upper floors. Bathrooms, a bar and billiard room on the east side were also added to the facility. It was opened for business in Nov 1919, with James Henry De Zilwa (1888–1979), a younger cousin of Ephraums, taking over as the Manager.

The hotel was used by the British, during World War II, as a Rest and Recuperation facility for servicemen. The property was then sold to Gerald 'Gem' Milhuisen in the 60s, when the owners migrated to Australia. The place is now managed and run by the Jetwings Hotel Group.

Lake Gregory

Lake Gregory, also referred to as Gregory Lake or Gregory Reservoir, is a large pool of water in the heart of Nuwara Eliya town. It was constructed during the British rule of **Governor Sir William Gregory** in 1873.

Sir William Gregory became the governor of Nuwara Eliya in 1872 and further developed the town into a place of beauty and typical English climate and atmosphere, and, was also instrumental in building Gregory Lake from a swamp to what is today known as Gregory Lake.

He also gave the message to world that Nuwara Eliya was an ideal place for agriculture, especially for coffee, Tea, Cinkona and animal farming.

The lake and the surrounding area make up the Gregory Lake Area. The area was originally a swampy **bog** at the foot of the small hills that border the town.

In 1873 Sir William Gregory authorised the damming of the Thalagala stream, which originates from Mount **Pidurutalagala**, in order to make more land available for the expansion of the town. In 1881 the lake was stocked with trout by CJR Le Mesurier (Assistant Government Agent for Nuwara Eliya).

In 1913 the waters of the lake were directed into a tunnel which flows to a hydro power station at 'Blackpool' between the town and **Nanu Oya**. The power station continues to supply electricity to the town to this day. In **British times** Lake Gregory was used for water sports and recreational activities.

In 1877 Sir Robert London became the Governor of Nuwara Eliya, and was instrumental in building the railway track from Peradeniya to Nawalapitiya and then from there to Hatton and Nanu Oya.

People fished for trout in Lake Gregory. (No boat rides and walkways were available then)

"Kachcheri" (District Secretariat)

The Kachcheri was completely destroyed by a fire in 1994

"Single Tree Hill Buddhist Temple"

Located on Single Tree Hill just south of the town this temple is located at a height of 6,890 ft (2,100m) above sea level. The significance and the reason for the peak to obtain the name Single tree Hill Buddhist temple is because the peak has just one tree on top of it. It is quite a view since the hill has just a beautiful tree and a magnificent temple.

"Holy Trinity Church"

The Holy Trinity Church, located on Church Road, belonging to "The Church of England", designed to resemble Canterbury Cathedral, was initiated in 1833 and the building, constructed according to typical English architecture, was only completed by 1843. The church was officially declared open on Feb 24 1852. It served as the principal place of worship for the Christian communities who lived in the town.

Several notable English planters are built in the cemetery. Some of the notables are Dr G Gardner, Superintendent of the Royal Botanical Gardens in Peradeniya, John Garland Baker, brother of Sir Samuel Baker, Eliza Heberden Baker, wife of John Garland, founder of the Baker Ward in the hospital, Captain William Fisher, father of Lord Fisher, RB Downall, later representative to the Legislative Council, Lady Ridgeway, wife of Sir West Ridgeway, (Governor of Ceylon), and Lady Olive Mary Caldecotte, wife of Sir Andrew Caldecotte, the last Governor of old Ceylon.

Other personalities buried in these precincts are Edwin Arthur Bartholomeusz, Edwin Sproule, Alfred Scott Berwick, Lieutenant JA Cantlay, Neander Warburtom Davies, Reginald Beauchamp Downall, Victor Ferne Edwards, Richard Christopher Elliott, Thomas Farr, Conrad Francis William Fisher, Harry Payne Gallway, Dr George Gardner, Thomas Wilkonson Hardstaff MBE FCA, Captain Henry Helsham, Reginald Huysheh Elliot, William Maxwell Kelly, Angus Llewellyn Lewis, John Mactier, Algernon Nelson Paine, Hamilton Mansfield Paterson, Herbert Henry Phelp, & Reverend Lucien Augustine Philipps.

"Al Kabeer Jumuah Mosque"

Located on Hill Street, the Mosque was established in 1935 for the benefit of the Muslim residents and visitors to the town to perform their prayers and religious obligations.

Nuwara Eliya Market"

The Market was always crowded with people who were buying their daily provisions of fruits, veggies, dry rations and meats.

People took off from Colombo, lock stock and barrel, to stay for a month or more during the "April Season" which afforded a break from steaming summer sun in the capital.

Many had their own bungalows and some would rent. Most of the house help were also taken along, as well. It was very much a family outing for most city dwellers.

No doubt, it was an era of gracious living for the rich, famous, and elite. The horse races were very much a focal point. They also had beautifully manicured gardens and vegetable plots around the racecourse.

The Planters Club and the Golf Club were where many of these folk hung out and enjoyed their time mingling with a similar bunch of people.

Vegetables were grown commercially only by vegetable farmers. Meat was mostly managed by butchers who belonged to the Indian Moor community.

The Golf Club, an 18 hole course, located on Badulla Road, is one of the oldest golf clubs in Sri Lanka which was established in the late 19 century.

Constructed in 1889 by a Scottish soldier. belonging to the Gordon Highlanders, the club served as a recreation center for the British servicemen and other officials stationed in Nuwara Eliya. Initially the course had 9 holes and was later upgraded to 18 holes in 1893. A Golf pavilion was also constructed in 1892. Many local golf tournaments and events are still conducted at the club much to the glee of golf enthusiasts.

The extent of the golf course is around 40.5 hectares (100 acres) and is located at an elevation of 1,830m (6,000 ft) above sea level.

The club, today, boasts of over 2,000 members.

"The Park"

The Nuwara Eliya Park is located in town adjacent to the Post Office. It was, originally, the research field of the Hakgala Botanical Gardens.

The park was named, formally as Victoria Park, to mark the Diamond Jubilee of Queen Victoria in 1897.

The Nanu Oya river cuts through the park creating many small lakes and ponds within its facility. Many rare bird species are found to nest in the park.

"The Bazaar"

The Bale Bazaar in Nuwara Eliya, located on New Bazaar Street, is so named because it offers the customers a wide range of warm clothes and woolens of various well-known brands. It offered a wide range of goods and services to the planter population as well as the residents and visitors to the town.

Tea

Little England - Located in Pedro Estate, Moonplains, is a residential location in Nuwara Eliya that got its name because of the fair skin of the people who lived in it.

Horton Plains

Horton Plains was originally referred to as Maha Eliya Thenna ("great open plain"). It was renamed by the British after Sir Robert William Horton, governor of Ceylon 1831-1837.

Horton Plains was designated as a wild life sanctuary in 1969. The extent of the land covered the Plains is 3,160 hectares (12.2 sq. mi). Horton Plains contains the most extensive area of cloud forest still existing in Sri Lanka.

Horton Plains is located on the southern plateau of the central highlands of Sri Lanka. The mountain peaks of Kirigalpotha (2,389m/7,838ft) and Thotupala Kanda (2,357m/7,733ft), the second and third highest mountains in Sri Lanka are situated to the west and north, respectively.

The park's **elevation** ranges from 1,200–2,300 metres (3,900–7,500 ft). The rocks found in the park belong to the Archaean age.

Moon Plains

Bambarakelle SOS Village

SOS Children's Village is located on 2.5 acres of land at Bambarakelle, Nuwara Eliya (180 km from Colombo), in

the central hill country of Sri Lanka. It is 6,283 feet above sea level, with the coldest climate in the country.

The village was inaugurated in April 1984 after the conflict between the Tamil Tigers and the government in 1983. The facility brings children of both communities together, here, to live as one family.

At SOS Children's Village Nuwara Eliya a total of ten families, six Sinhala and four Tamil were established, originally. A strong and united SOS Family has been built here in order to foster amity and unity between the people.

Shops, Stores & Business Houses

Abdul Rahims, a wholesaler for all types of household goods, was first established, in Galle in 1872, by ILM Mohamed Cassim. The company then expanded to Colombo. The Kandy and Nuwara Eliya branches were inaugurated in 1930.

Abraham Saibo Estate Suppliers were the pioneer hardware trading establishment in the town. They also ran a butchers stall.

Cargills has been the largest department store in the town of Nuwara Eliya since the 60s. Established in Colombo in 1844 the store has catered to the Colonial British and the upper middle class local community in the island. Planters, living in the hill stations, visited this store to buy their provisions. They offered everything from vegetables, fruits, frozen food, meats, dairy, to Sweaters and warm clothing.

William Milne, a British businessman, started 'Milne & Company' in 1844. The company was engaged in general warehousing, and also importers of oilman stores, canned food, and dairy products from the UK.

Milne was joined by his friend, David Sime Cargill, in in 1850 and the firm changed its name to 'Milne, Cargill & Co'. Milne retired from the business in Ceylon and moved back to Scotland in 1860 and formed a company in Glasgow to manage the business of Cargill & Co in Ceylon.

Cargill, then, became the sole partner until he was joined by David MacKenzie, and the name of the store was changed to 'Cargill & Co'.

The company had its Colombo office at the intersection of Price and York Streets in the Fort of Colombo. Branches were then opened in Kandy, at Upper Lake Road, and an office in the Fort of Galle, at 22 Pedlar Street. The Galle office was closed in 1863.

In 1890 the business expanded with the purchase of 'Medical Hall,' a chemist and druggist company. Cargills also established another company, 'Sime & Co.' which sold lower quality goods.

In 1896 Cargill & Co. was converted into a Limited Liability Company registered in Glasgow.

Two years later, the company bought James McLaren &Co.'s business in Nuwara Eliya, establishing a branch in the hill station.

Gunadasa & Company, on Lawson Street is an auto and spare parts dealer.

Chandirams, a leading gents tailoring establishment.

Favourites, is located on New Bazaar Street

Ceylon Motors

Edmund Stores

Fountain Hardware

Paul Soris & Company

S. T. SORIS, THE PEDRO VIEW HOTEL, THE VEGETABLE GARDEN, AND INTERIOR OF THE STORE.

This firm was established in a small provision store at Nuwara Eliya in the year 1869 by Mr Paul Soris, a native of Tuticorin in South India. The business increased rapidly and Mr Soris was succeeded by Mr ST Soris, his oldest son. They engage in imports of goods from England and Europe, as well as dealing with large commercial houses in Colombo in Ceylon.

Their vegetable gardens cover ten acres and the seeds that are sown here are imported directly from England and Australia.

The company has won thirty two prizes for their high quality vegetables at the local agro horticultural exhibitions and shows. They are represented in London by Ms Service Reeve & Company.

Twentieth Century Impressions of Ceylon by Arnold Wright

Green Gables

Jacob Stores

John & Company

The Municipal Tour Inn

K A Meera Sahibo & Sons

KP Butani (Butanis) A corporate establishment run by the Butani family whose sons are Prakash, Ranjit, Kishin & Raj.

Malika Stores (opposite the market)

Nandias

New Trivoli Cinema

PMM Zahir (Zahir Sons)

Regal Cinema

Selvasingh

Star Hotel & Bakery

Vadivel Brothers (close to Cargills)

Woodland Hotel

Yusuf Stores, located on New Bazaar Road is now a large clothing department store, named Gunatex.

People

Ralph George Carte AMICE

The Hon JM Campbell

Donald Mcinlay Murray

Frank Grenier

Barbara Layard

MU Leembruggen

Charles Ryan

JPE Ryan

Barbara Jane Layard

Twentieth Century Impressions of Ceylon by Arnold Wright

pp825-826

Plantations

Inverness, established in 1880 was owned by GM Ballardie until 1888 when it was sold to AL Cross who owned it until 1892. The management then passed on to E Mack, who ran the facility from 1891-92.

Inverness is the selling mark for Nuwara Eliya Estate

Elephant Nook, was established in 1887 and was owned by WR Tringham who managed it until 1893. The Nuwara Eliya Tea Estate Company then took over the place and ran it from 1909 to 1914.

The Estate was managed by Tringham, WE Glenie, ACW Ferguson, and CT Nettleton until 1914.

Mahagastotte, established in 1891 by Ms JG Baker and Captain JA Baker, and their descendants until 1930.

Warwick, established in 1880/81 by WJ Cotton.

Pedro, 1880 by Capt. F Bailey

Cornwall, established in 1884 was owned and managed by Mark Kellow and his heirs until 1886. It was then managed by Duncan Muliens, FHA Foster, and the Kellow family until 1893.

Naseby, was established in 1883 by Ms C Ferguson and continued to do business under her family until 1912.

Heathersett, owned by J MacAndrew, was established in 1883 and managed by English planters until 1921.

Gallebodde was established in 1887 and managed by the Colombo Commercial Company.

Bambarakelle, was established in 1880 by GF Trail.

Oliphant, established by GHD Elphinstone in 1880.

Court Lodge, established in 1880 by E & A Delmege.

Pidurutalagala Mountain

Pidurutalagala (*Straw Plateau Rock*), or **Mount Pedro** in English, is an ultra-prominent peak and the tallest mountain in Sri Lanka, towering 2,524 m (8,281 ft). It is situated North-North-East from the town of Nuwara Eliya and is clearly visible from most areas of the Central region. Presently, the summit is home to the central communications array of the Sri Lankan government and armed forces, and, serves as an important location in the country's radar communication system.

Kukulegala Mountain Range

The Kukulegala mountain range is a beautiful environment that nature endowed to Sri Lanka. The peak is 1,531 meters high and is considered as the boundary between the Nuwara Eliya and Kandy districts.

It is located near the town of Rikillagaskada. Towering over the Wilpassa Lake, this mountain range creates a unique ecosystem where a large animal community live.

The village folk believe that the place is called Kukulegala because a rooster came and crowed on top of it. "Kukula" = Rooster, "Gala" = Rock, in Sinhala,

Ambewela Farm

Spanning 150 acres, the Ambewela Farm is a popular dairy farm for its well-known products. Here, the cows roam free, grazing on the green pastures of the farm, and the sky is almost always crystal blue. With wind turbines dotting the scenery in the distance, the peaceful farm is a great place to visit away from the hustle and bustle of the cities.

The farm was initially started with the help of the New Zealand government in the '60s, and besides producing milk, yoghurt, cream, and cheese, the farm is also a popular destination in Nuwara Eliya for tourists and locals alike.

Vegetable Gardens

Strawberry Farm

Waterfalls

Lovers Leap

Schools

Good Shepherd BMV Nuwaraeliya
N/Court Lodge TV Kandapola
Talawakelle PMV Talawakele
Ragala T B M Herath Maha Vidyalaya
Ragala Tamil MV
St Mary's TMV Bogawantalawa
Dharmakeerthy Sinhala MV Bogawantalawa
St Joseph's TMV Maskeliya
Batagolla Pussadewa MMV Walapane
Padiyapelella Maha Vidyalaya Padiyapelella
Keerthi Bandara MV
Lyceum International College
Poramadulla Central College
Diyathilaka Central College
Our Ladys School

St Edward's School

This is a well-known educational establishment, started in 1888, which enjoys a well deserved reputation the the town of Nuwara Eliya. It constituted mainly of children belonging to British families who lived and served in the town.

Many were the students who came from different parts of the country and even from India, to benefit from the quality of the education and discipline that was offered at this institution.

The school was started by JEB Brine in the locality in order to provide a first grade education to the children of the European families.

Mr Brine retired at the end of 1898 and the management passed on to HH Phelph, MA Durham, assisted by an efficient staff comprising ET David, BA London.

The establishment is sponsored by the Government and well cared for in all its needs. The buildings are very spacious and stand on 10 acres of land. It also occupies one of the best sites in the town of Nuwara Eliya and has the advantage of being afforded an abundant supply of pure drinking water.

The boys are also offered the facility of the Nuwara Eliya Cricket Club which is located a short walk from the school premises.

Twentieth Century Impressions of Ceylon by Arnold Wright pp833

St Edwards Bungalow

Demographics

Sinhalese 45%

Sri Lankan Tamil 22%

Indian Tamil 21%

Moor 10.5%

Others 1.5%

Weather – Record highs & lows

Jan 32.2C/-2.6C

Feb 31.7C/=-2.5C

Mar 33.9C/-1.9C

Apr 29.9C/0.8C

May 32.5C/0.8C

Jun 27.6C/6.4C

Jul 29.2C/6.0C

Aug 29.8C/5.1C

Sep 25.8C/5.0C

Oct 27.6C/1.2C

Nov 28.6C/1.4C

Dec 27.5C/-1.1C

Towns within the Nuwara Eliya District

Hapugastalawa
Agrapatana
Ambewela
Bogawantalawa
Bopattalawa
Dayagama Bazaar
Ginigathena
Haggala
Hanguranketha
Hatton-Dikoya UC
Kotagala
Kotmale
Labukele
Laxapana
Lindula-Talawakele UC
Maskeliya
Nildandahinna
Nuwara Eliya
Nanu Oya
Norton Bridge
Padiyapelella
Ramboda
Ragala
Rikillagaskada
Rozella
Udapussallawa
Walapane
Watawala
Norton
Koththallena
Pundaluoya
Kandapola
Pattipola

Udarata Menike

The Udarata Menike (country maiden) is a passenger train that runs from Colombo to the hill stations in the central province.

The train made its maiden journey on 23 April 1956.

The Udarata Menike begins its eastbound service from Colombo Fort station and runs east and north past the centers of Ragama, Gampaha, Veyangoda, Polgahawela. At Rambukkana, the main line begins its steep climb up to the hills of tea country.

Podi Menike

"Podi Menike" ("Little Maiden") is a passenger train running from Colombo Fort to Badulla. The journey covers about 300 km and is renowned for being the most beautiful stretch of train journey in Sri Lanka, especially the stretch from Nanu Oya to Ella. It takes about 10 hours to complete the whole journey.

The train follows the up country line route developed by the British, similar to the Udarata Menike, in the 19th century through scenic mountains. The route features bridges, long tunnels, high slopes and gradients.

Bus/Taxi Service

One can also travel to Nuwara Eliya by bus or taxi from the main bus station at Pettah in Colombo and also from other cities across the island.

The bus ride usually takes 6 hours and one can make it in less by riding a private taxi can.

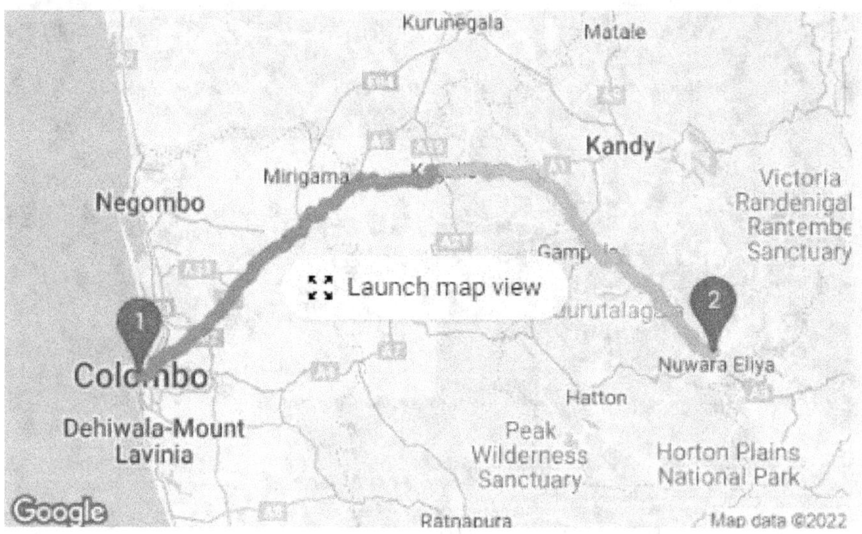

Bus/Taxi route

Luxury private bus service

Sri Lanka Transport Board public bus service

Ode to Nuwara Eliya

Rail me back to Nuwara Eliya,

There's where the tea and the pears and berries grow.

There's where the streams trickle sweet in the springtime.

There's where the mist in the morning hangs low.

Drive me round the vast open spaces,

There's where the dairy and the meat and veggies grow.

There's where the horses neigh snorting in the sunshine.

There's where the flowers bloom brightly from their bough.

Walk me up old Piduru-tala-gala,

There's where the fauna and the wily old fox roams.

There's where the rocks are hewn all over nature.

There's where true peace reigns calm in our home.

Take me down to the lush green Plains.

There's where the birds and the bees and fauna go.

There's where the world seems to end in its lifetime.

There's where the beauty of life seems to flow.

mellia

SRI LANKA POLICE - NUWARAELIYA
POST OFFICE

History

http://nuwaraeliyainfo.com/information/history

The history of Nuwara Eliya roughly dates back to 1818 when Dr. John Davy discovered Nuwara Eliya as a place with a similar climate as England and also a place full of wild animals for hunting such as Elephants, and other animals and also full of Asoka trees. When the Uwa Wellassa battle was raging at this time the British had established themselves in the Kothmale area. The British then ventured out for hunting as a hobby and then suddenly found themselves in an area where the climate was very similar to England.

The original Nuwara Eliya was a patina with no trees or greenery. It is suspected that the reason for this was that there was a fire during the Ramayana where Hunuman set fire to the region.

Since the present Nuwsara Eliya soil is black in colour it is believed that this is due to the fore that took place during the Rama/ Rawana war. The traveler Iban Bathuththa discovered "Adam's Peak: and found a plant named "Rathambara" (Ma Ratmal) which was a medicinal plant. It was found that this plant was resistant to fire and therefore did not catch fire Therefore it can be believed that when the original fire took place only this particular plant survived the fire.

Sir Edward Barnes, governor from 1824 to 1831 built his home known as "Barnes Hall" which is today called the Grand Hotel.

From 1831-1837 the governor was Sir William Horton who had written many articles about Nuwara Eliya in his many literary works In 1838, Samuel Baker, an explorer, discovered Nuwara Eliya as a place with the exact climate of England and made it into a retreat for the British colonists to retire and relax and indulge in hunting which as a favorite past time.

He also introduced farming during this time. Mr Baker was also instrumental in building "Baker's Farm, a hospital ward at the Nuwara Eliya base hospital known today as Bakers Ward.

He returned to England in 1866 due to ill health. However, recognition of his work at Nuwara Eliya the broadest water fall in Nuwara Eliya was named after him and is called " Bakers Falls:'

In 1872, Sir William Gregory became the governor of Nuwara Eliya and further developed Nuwara Eliya to a place of beauty and a typical English climate and atmosphere and was instrumental in building the Gregory Lake from a swamp to what is today known as Gregory Lake. He also gave the message to world that Nuwara

Eliya was an ideal place for agriculture and specially for coffee, Tea, Cinkona and animal farming.

In 1877, Sir Robert London became the Governor, who was instrumental in building the railway track from Peradeniya to Nawalapitiya, and then, from there, further, to Hatton and Nanu Oya.

People & Places

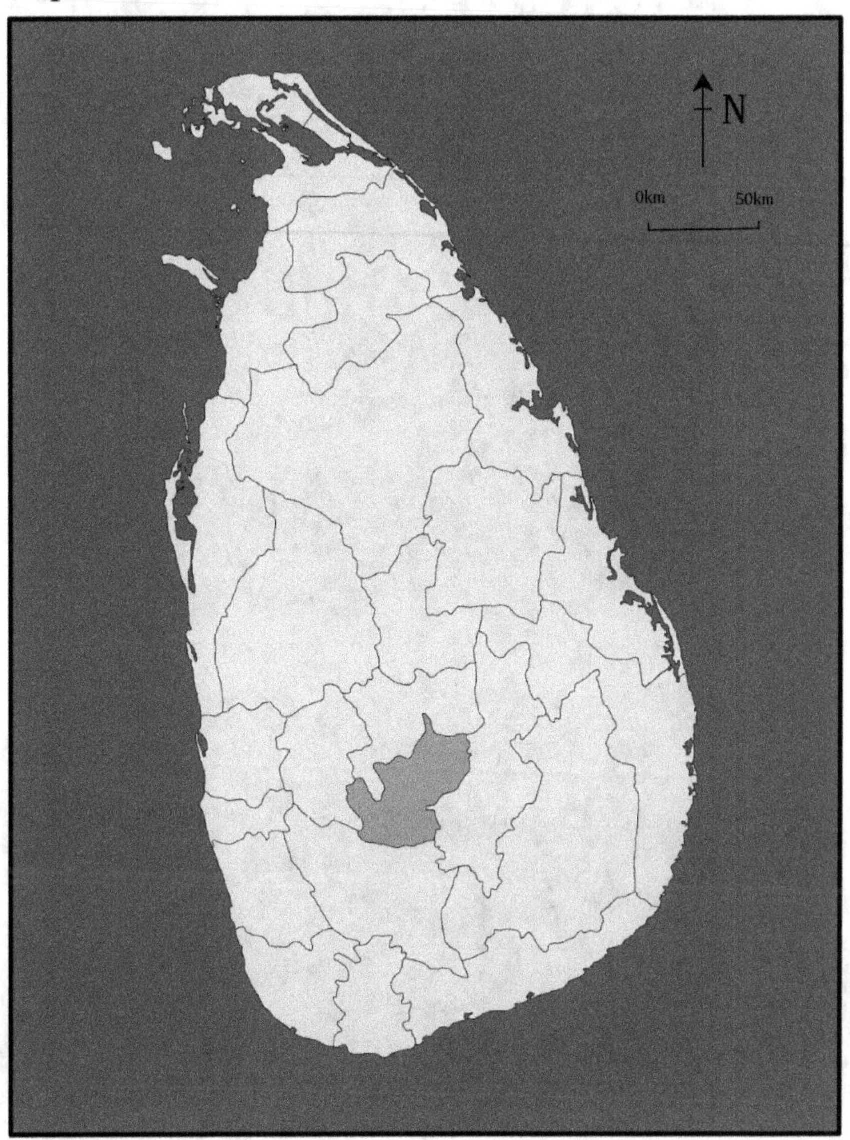

About the Author

Fazli Sameer was born, on 16 February, 1948, in Bambalapitiya, Colombo-4, and was educated in the English Medium at Royal Primary School (1953-58) and Royal College (1959-66), Colombo. In 1967/68 he spent the first year of the course in BSc. Physical Science at the University of Colombo and left thereafter to pursue a course in Computer Science with IBM.

His employment covered stints at Chartered Bank in Colombo (1979-89), Citibank in the Middle East (1979-1999), Al Faisaliah Group in Saudi Arabia (1999-2008) in Information Technology, and private Business & IT Consulting from 2008 to date.

Since 1979, Fazli has been engaged in researching, collecting, and publishing genealogy data of all Sri Lankan communities.
He published, Family Tree Data: Genealogical Tables of Sri Lankan Muslims in 1996, and manages the Sri Lanka Genealogy Website on the internet at the link:

http://www.worldgenweb.org/lkawgw

Fazli has also been researching, preserving and publishing the history and legacy of Sri Lankan people, places, and significant events. He writes and manages a blog, titled F's Place which contains valuable data of streets, people, homes, and families who lived in Colombo in the 1960s:
http://kermeey.blogspot.com

He is also into prose and poetry on his personal blog. F's Space: http://kermeey2.blogspot.com

He has been contributing to the English Writers Workshop, previously held at the Beach Wadiya, in Wellawatte, since January 2019.

Fazli married Shirani Ibrahim in 1974. They have two daughters, Melina & Nadia and two grandkids, Maria & Abdullah.

Reading and writing was always a great passion in the Sameer household in Bambalapitiya, in Colombo. Newspapers, magazines, and books were freely available, in abundance, for everyone to indulge in. The bookman, who rode all his novels on the back of a bike, was a regular visitor to the home.

Fazli is also the author of "Bamba Days" published in Aug 2020 which describes the people, streets, homes, families and events in the town of Bambalapitiya (Colombo 00400) in the 60s, and "Wellawatte Ways" in 2021.

He also published a collection of poetry titled "February Frolic" in 2020 and a collection of 14 volumes of Sri Lankan Muslim Family Genealogy, 18 volumes of Burgher Families, 14 volumes of Sinhalese Families, and 1 volume of Tamil Families in 2021/2. Sophie Akka & Somapala, an Autobiography, Islamic Inheritance Q&A are also some of his other works, available on Amazon KDP and mycloudreader.

ooOoo

"on a mountain, in a mansion, stands my love"

[Jim Reeves]